HAL•LEONARD®

GUITAR PLAY-ALONG

AUDIO
ACCESS
INCLUDED

VOL. 82

T0056174

ISBN 978-1-4234-3083-4

HAL•LEONARD®

Visit Hal Leonard Online at
www.halleonard.com

Contact us:
Hal Leonard
7777 West Bluemound Road
Milwaukee, WI 53213
Email: info@halleonard.com

In Europe, contact:
Hal Leonard Europe Limited
42 Wigmore Street
Marylebone, London, W1U 2RN
Email: info@halleonardeurope.com

In Australia, contact:
Hal Leonard Australia Pty. Ltd.
4 Lentara Court
Cheltenham, Victoria, 3192 Australia
Email: info@halleonard.com.au

GUITAR PLAY-ALONG

AUDIO ACCESS INCLUDED

CONTENTS

Bad Case of Loving You

Words and Music by John Moon Martin

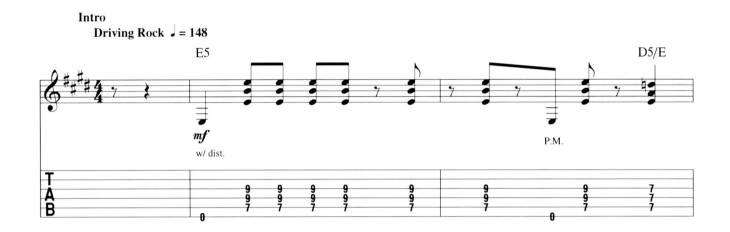

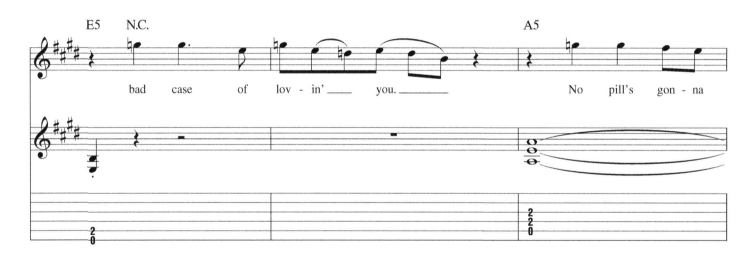

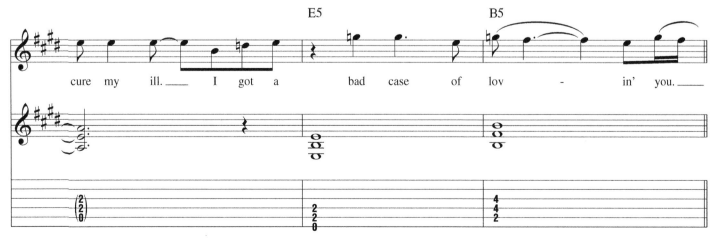

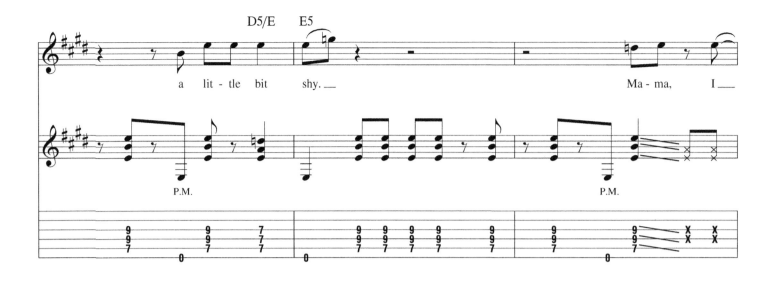

a lit - tle bit shy. ___ Ma - ma, I ___

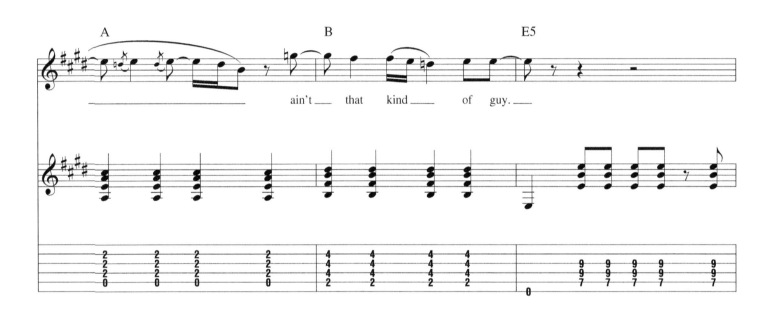

____ ain't ___ that kind ___ of guy. ___

Doc - tor, doc - tor, gim - me the news. ___ I got a

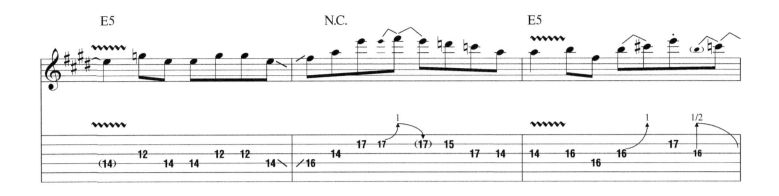

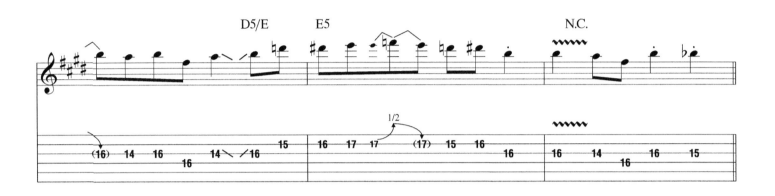

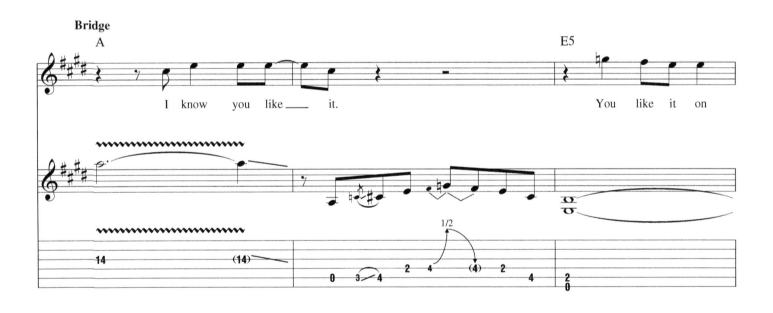

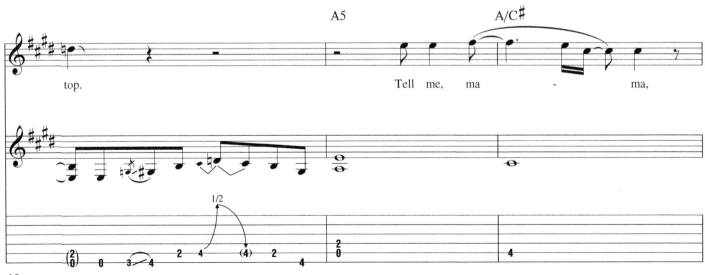

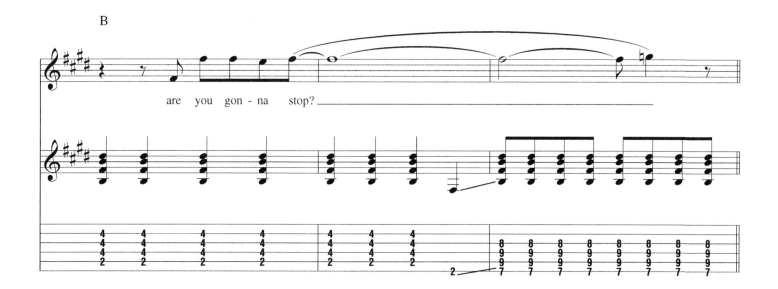

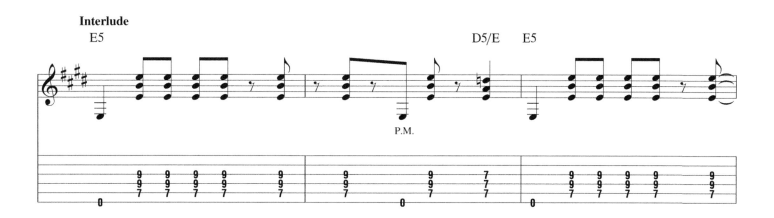

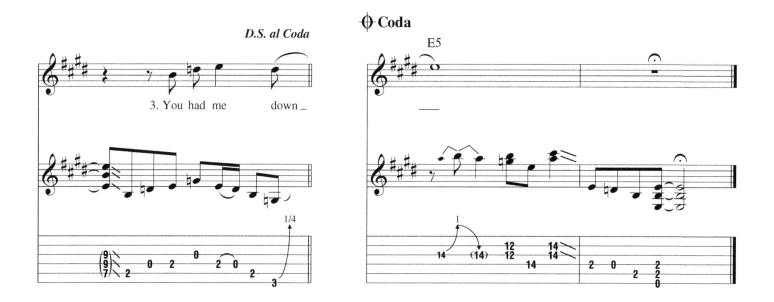

Additional Lyrics

3. You had me down, uh, twenty-one to zip,
   Smile of Judas on your lip.
   Shake my fist, knock on wood.
   I've got it bad and I got it good.

Bang a Gong (Get It On)

Words and Music by Marc Bolan

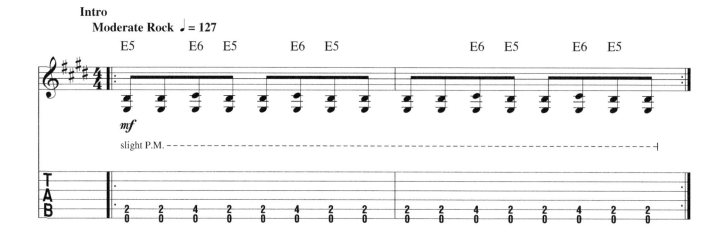

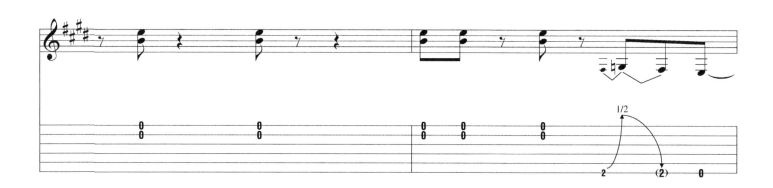

1. Well, you're dirt -

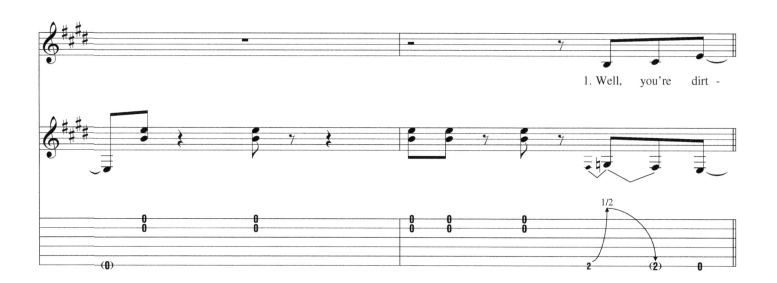

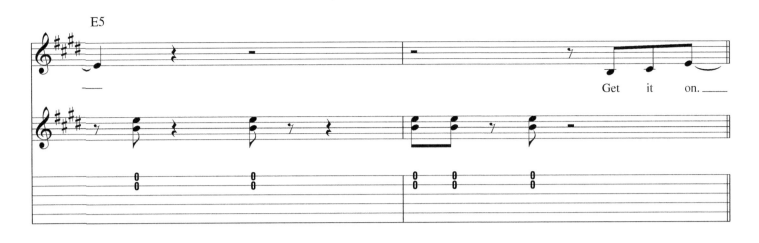

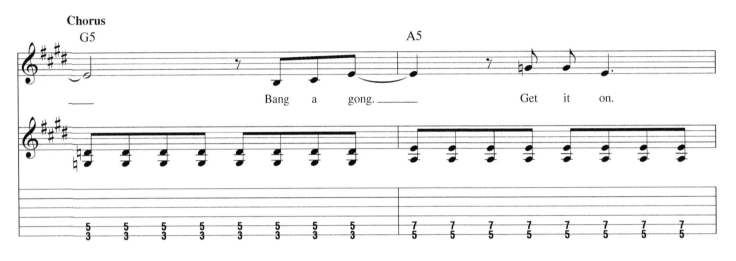

Chorus

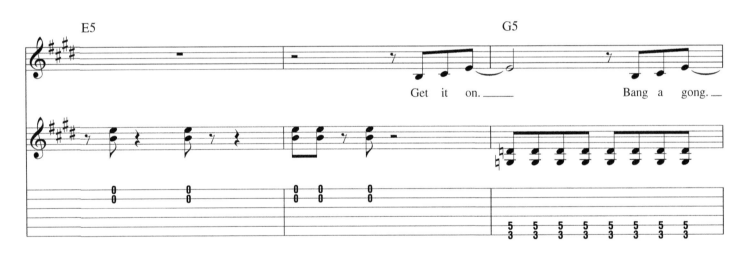

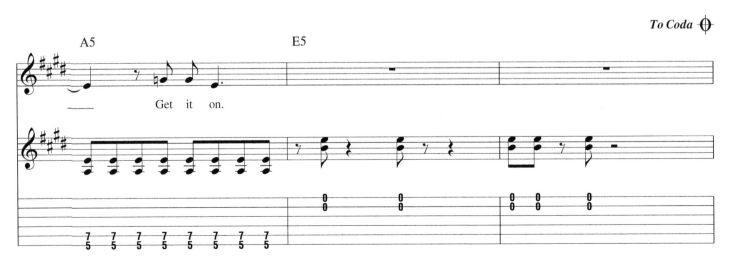

14

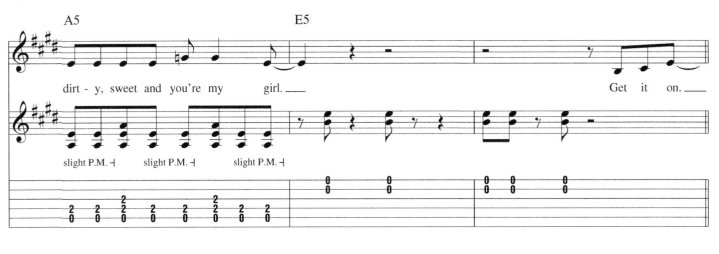

dirt - y, sweet and you're my girl. ___ Get it on. ___

slight P.M. ⊣ slight P.M. ⊣ slight P.M. ⊣

Chorus

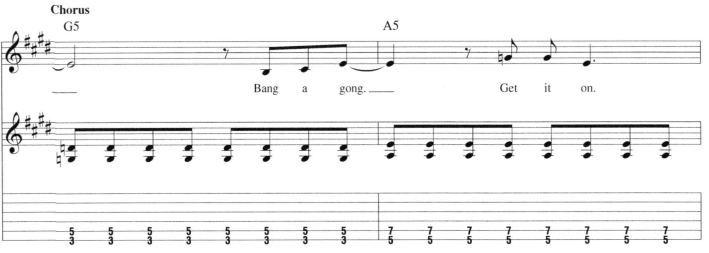

__ Bang a gong. ___ Get it on.

Get it on. ___ Bang a gong. __

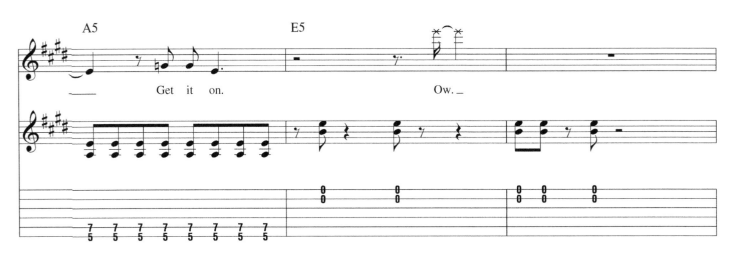

__ Get it on. Ow. _

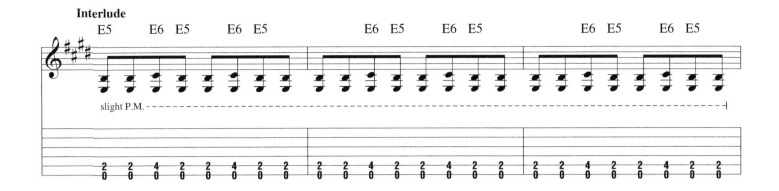

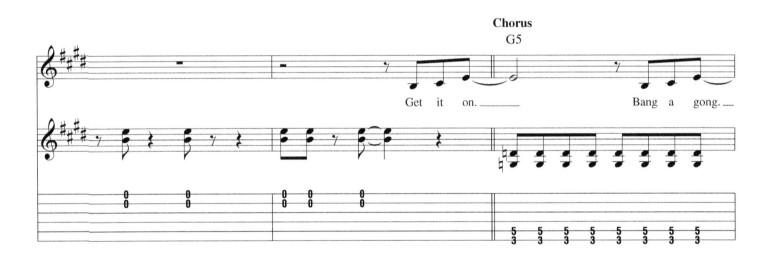

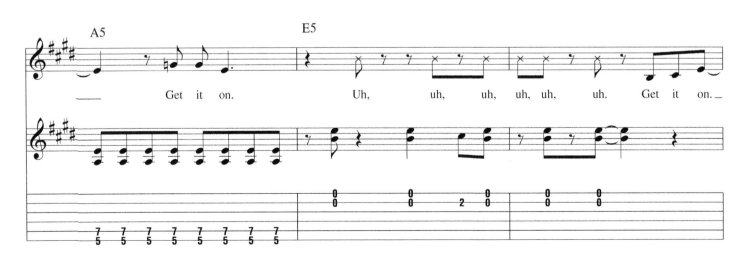

Outro

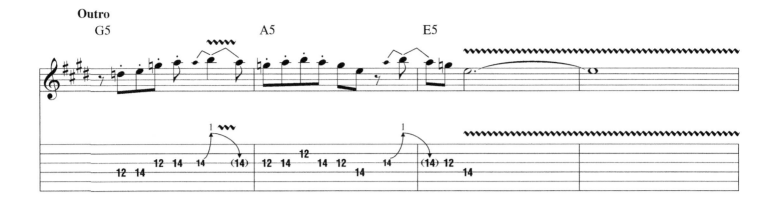

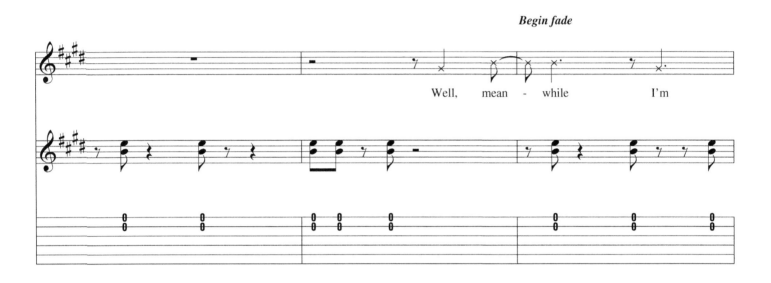

Well, mean - while I'm

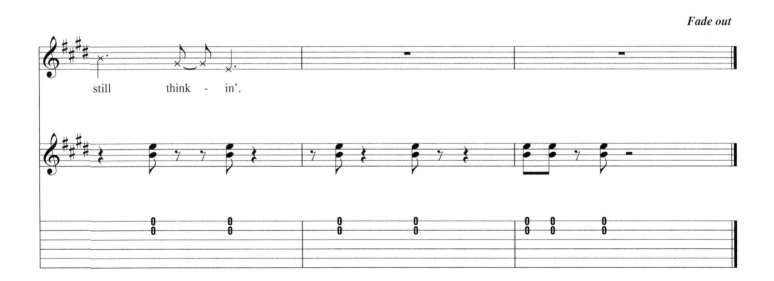

still think - in'.

Additional Lyrics

3. Well, you're windy and wild, you've got the blues in your shoes and your stockings.
   You're windy and wild, oh, yeah.
   Well, you're built like a car, you've got a hubcap diamond star halo.
   You're dirty, sweet and you're my girl.

I Love Rock 'N Roll

Words and Music by Alan Merrill and Jake Hooker

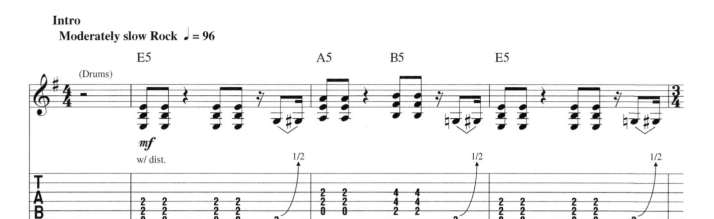

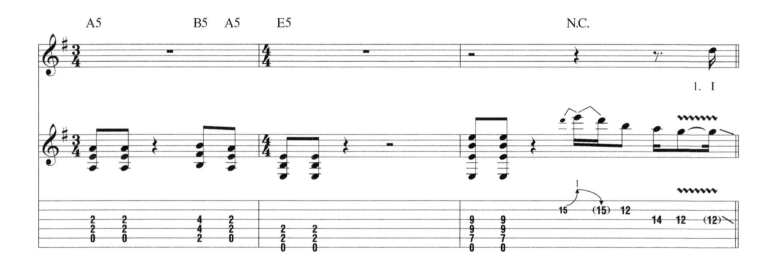

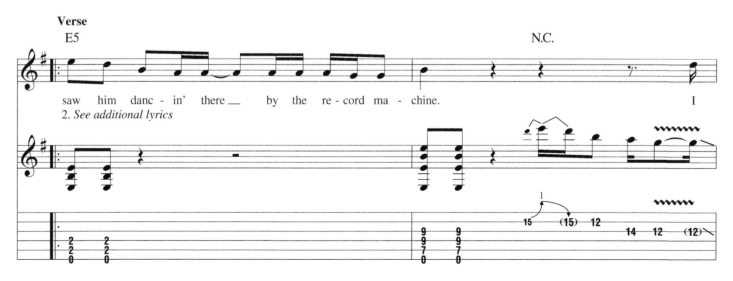

saw him danc-in' there ___ by the re-cord ma-chine.
2. *See additional lyrics*

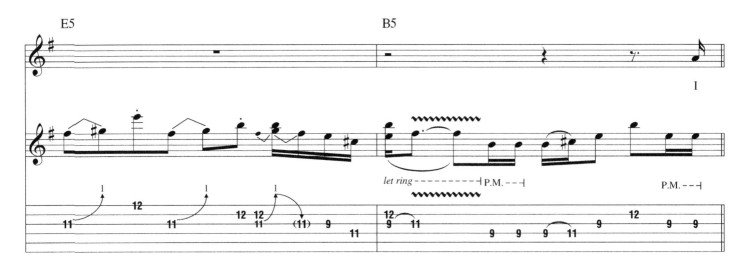

Pre-Chorus

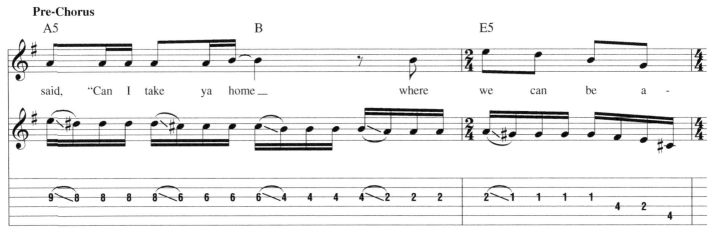

said, "Can I take ya home ___ where we can be a -

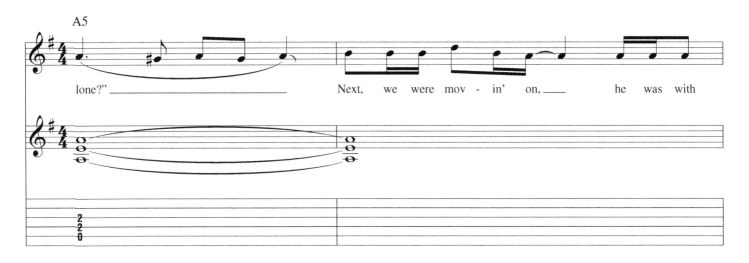

lone?" _____ Next, we were mov - in' on, ___ he was with

me, yeah, me! And we'll be mov - in' on, ___ and sing - in' that same old

Breakdown-Chorus

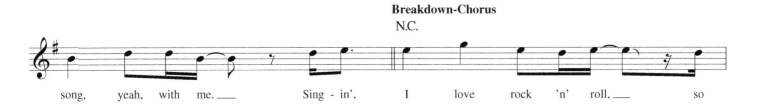

song, yeah, with me. ___ Sing - in', I love rock 'n' roll, ___ so

Outro-Chorus

Additional Lyrics

2. He smiled, so I got up and asked for his name.
"That don't matter," he said, "'cause it's all the same."
I said, "Can I take ya home where we can be alone?"
And next, we were movin' on, he was with me, yeah, me!
Next, we were movin' on, he was with me, yeah, me, singin',...

I Can't Explain

Words and Music by Peter Townshend

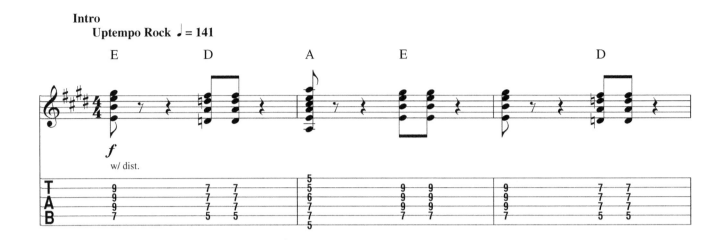

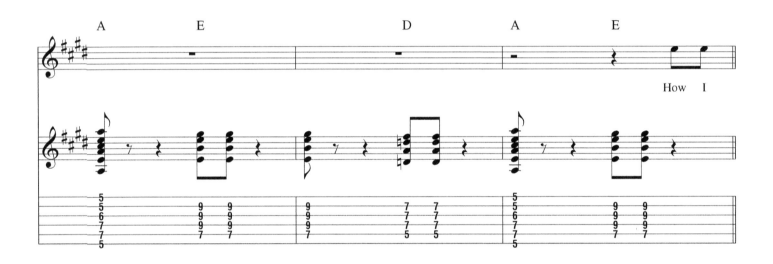

How I

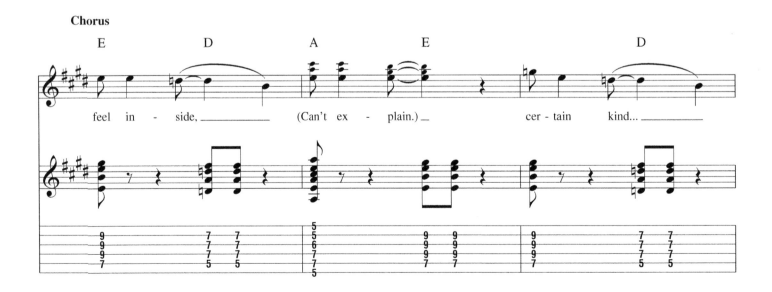

feel in - side, _____ (Can't ex - plain.) _____ cer - tain kind... _____

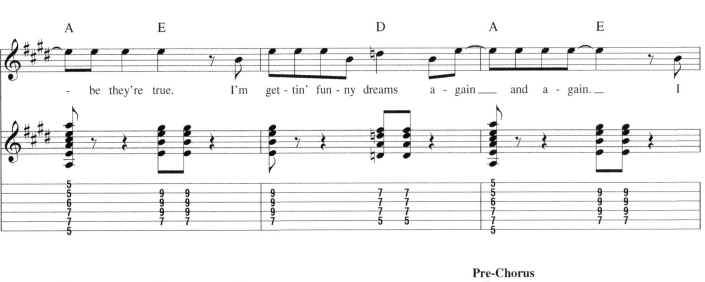

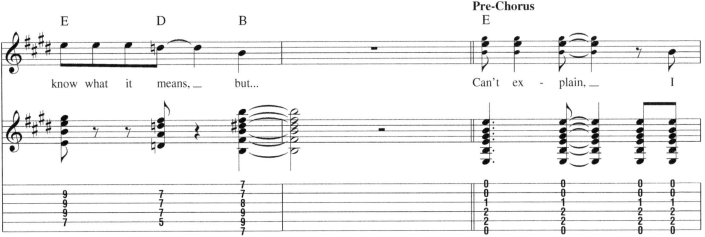

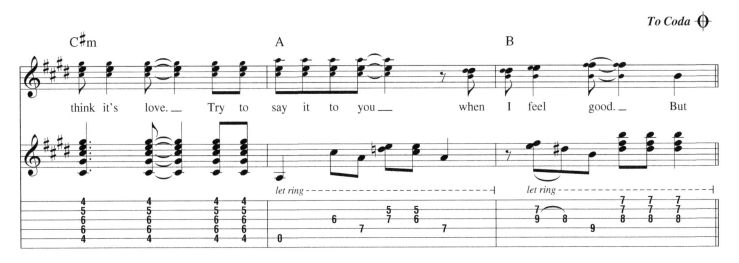

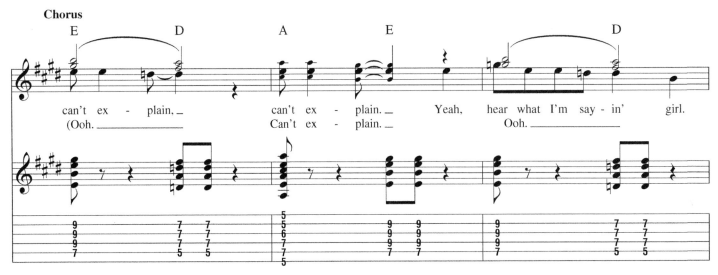

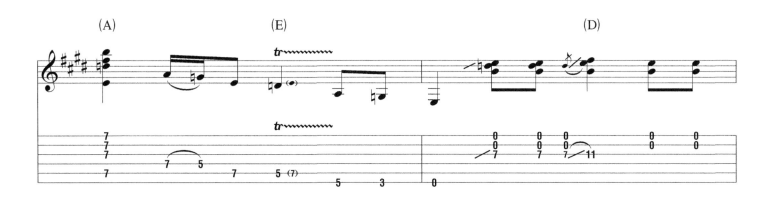

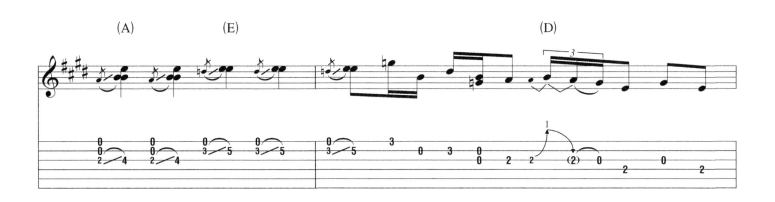

Chorus

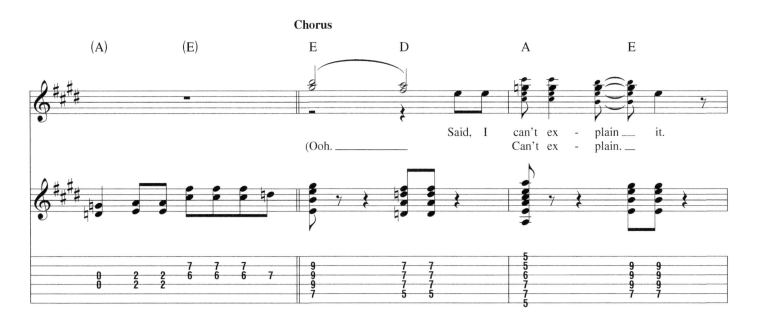

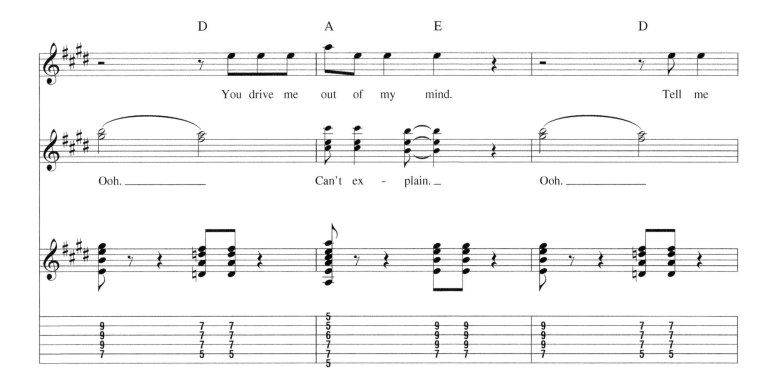

You drive me out of my mind. Tell me

Ooh. _____ Can't ex - plain. _____ Ooh. _____

what it's got ___ me, yeah. I said I can't ex - plain. ___

Can't ex - plain. ___ Ooh. _____ Can't ex - plain.) ___

Additional Lyrics

2. Dizzy in the head, and I feel bad.
The things you said got me real mad.
I'm gettin' funny dreams again and again.
I know what it means, but...

La Bamba

By Ritchie Valens

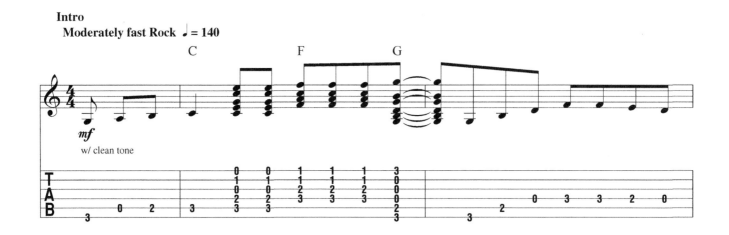

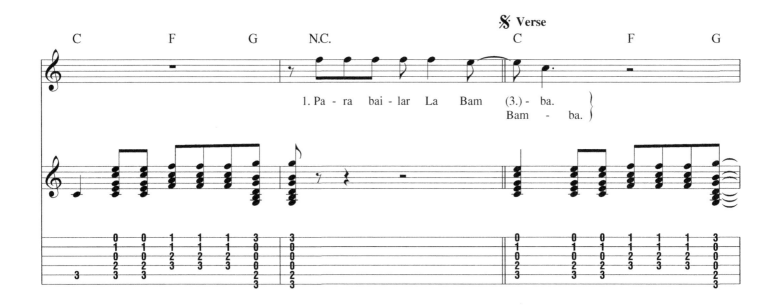

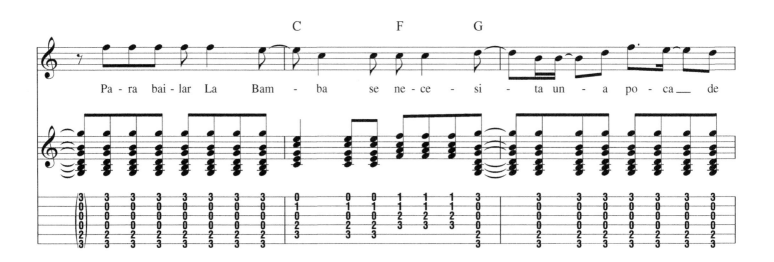

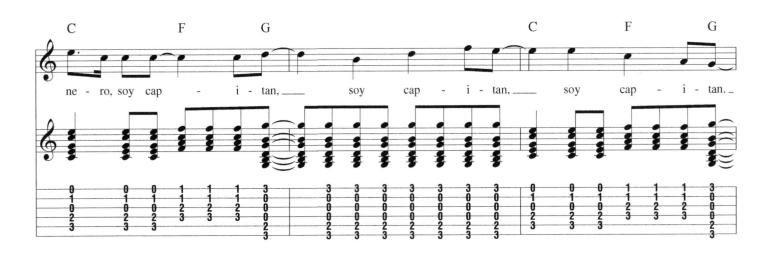

ne - ro, soy cap - i - tan, ____ soy cap - i - tan, ____ soy cap - i - tan. ____

Chorus

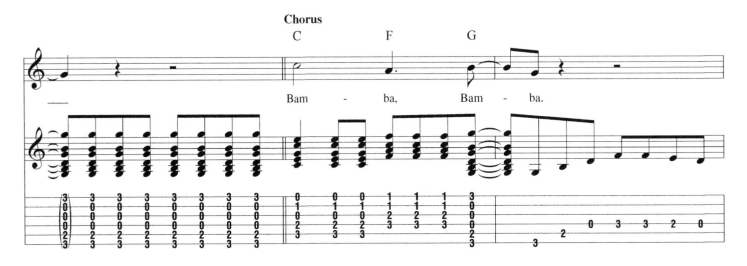

Bam - ba, Bam - ba.

Bam - ba, Bam - ba. Bam - ba, Bam -

D.S. al Coda 1

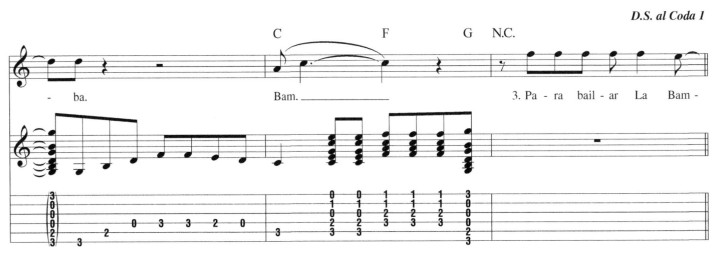

- ba. Bam. _____ 3. Pa - ra bail - ar La Bam -

Guitar Solo

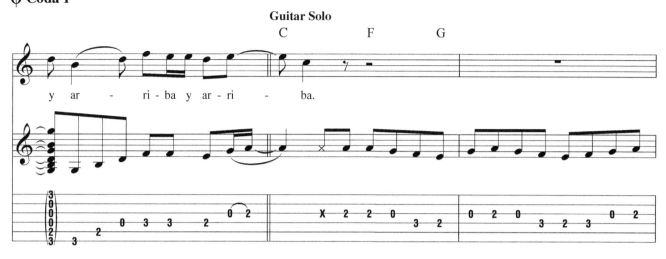

y ar - ri - ba y ar - ri - ba.

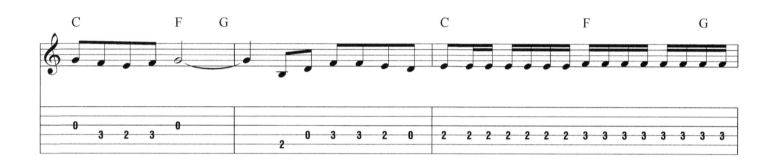

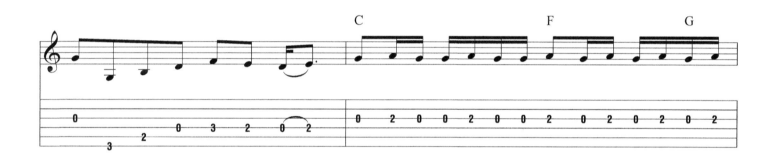

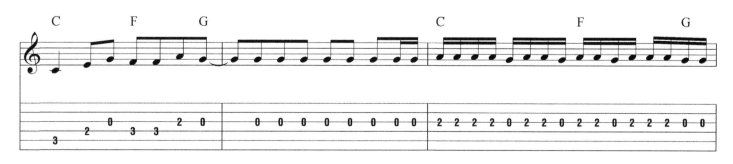

D.S. al Coda 2   **Coda 2**

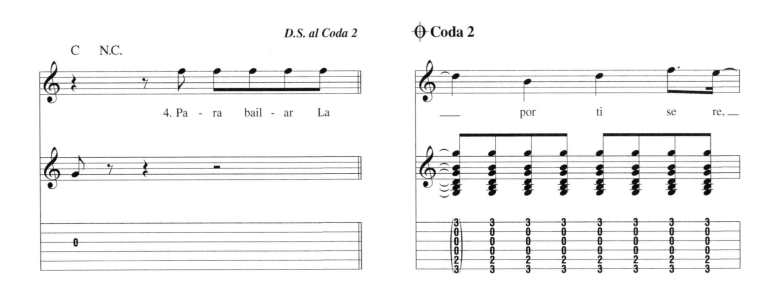

4. Pa - ra bail - ar La

— por ti se re, —

Outro-Chorus

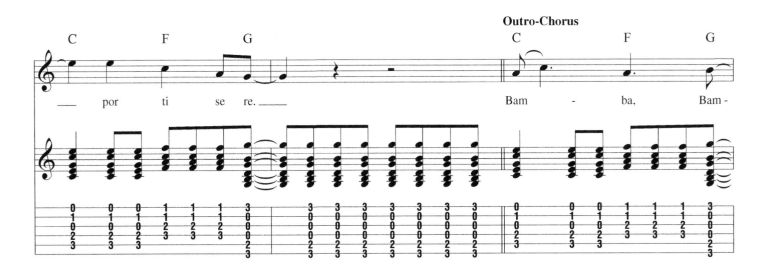

— por ti se re. —— Bam - ba, Bam -

Repeat and fade

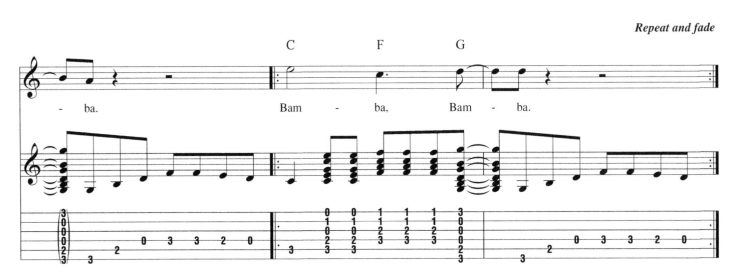

- ba. Bam - ba, Bam - ba.

Should I Stay or Should I Go

Words and Music by Mick Jones and Joe Strummer

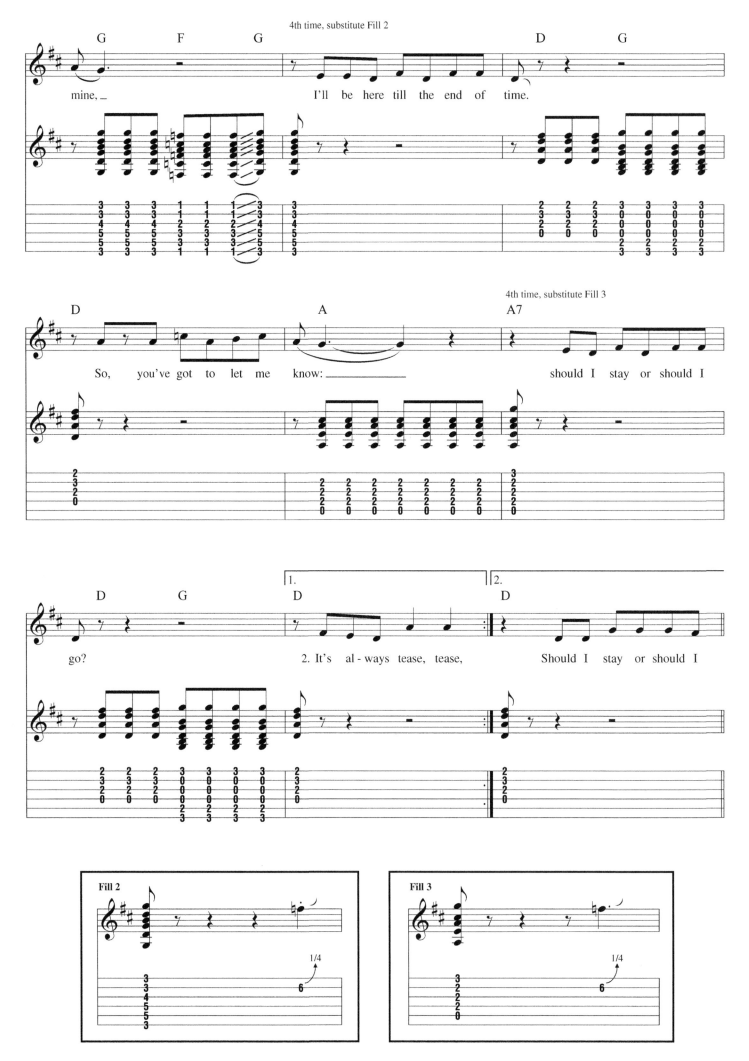

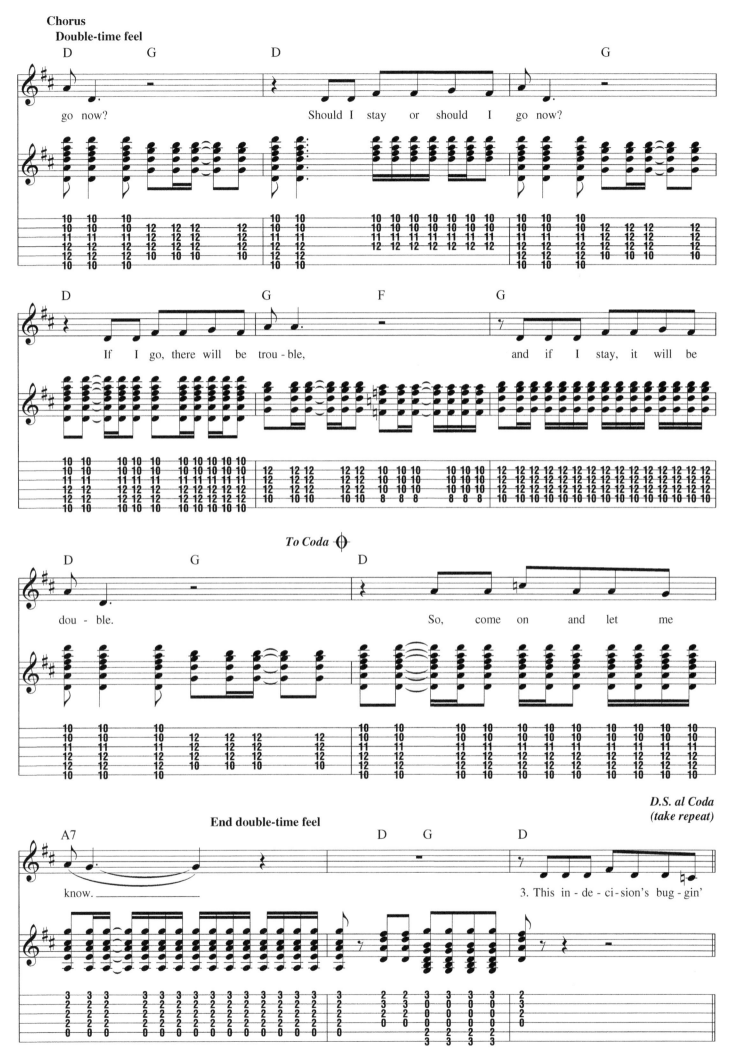

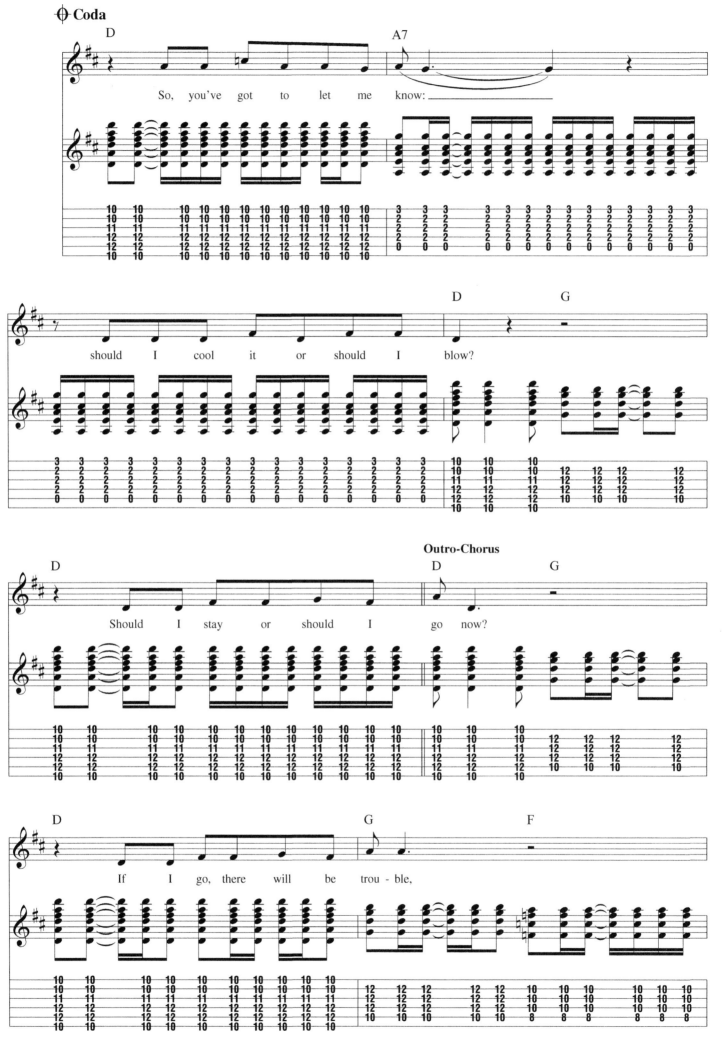

Additional Lyrics

2. It's always tease, tease, tease.
   You're happy when I'm on my knees.
   One day is fine and next it's black.
   So if you want me off your back,
   Well, come on and let me know:
   Should I stay or should I go?

3. This indecision's buggin' me.
   If you don't want me, set me free.
   Exactly who I'm s'pose to be?
   Don't you know which clothes even fit me?
   Come on and let me know:
   Should I cool it or should I blow?

4. *Instrumental*

Mony, Mony

Words and Music by Bobby Bloom, Tommy James, Ritchie Cordell and Bo Gentry

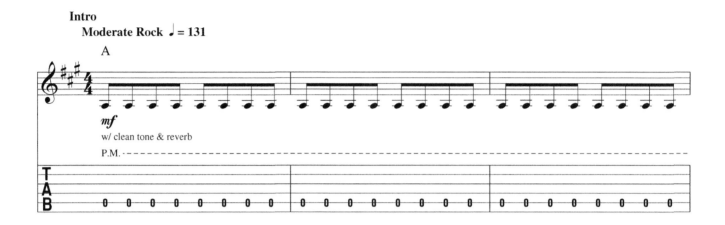

1. Here _____ she come now, say-in', "Mo-ny, Mo-ny." _____
2. *See additional lyrics*

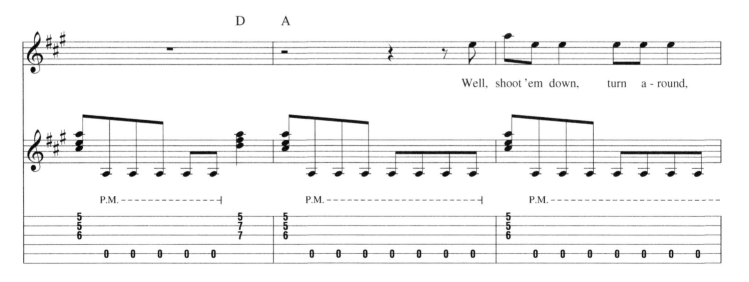

Well, shoot 'em down, turn a-round,

So fine. __
- ny. Ooh, __ I love ya Mo - ny, Mo - Mo - Mo - ny.

Al - right. __
Ooh, __ I love ya

E   D   D♯   E

Say,   Mo - ny,   Mo - ny.   Yeah, __   ev - 'ry - bod -
Mo - ny,   Mo - ny.   Yeah, __

D   D♯   E

y,   y - yeah, __   yeah, __   yeah, __   yeah. __
yeah, __   yeah,   yeah,   wah!)

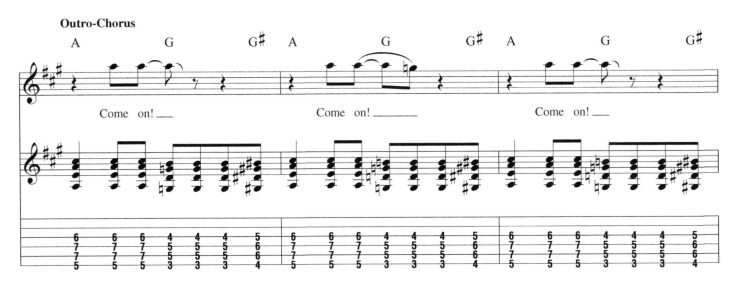

Outro-Chorus

A   G   G♯   A   G   G♯   A   G   G♯

Come on! __   Come on! _____   Come on! __

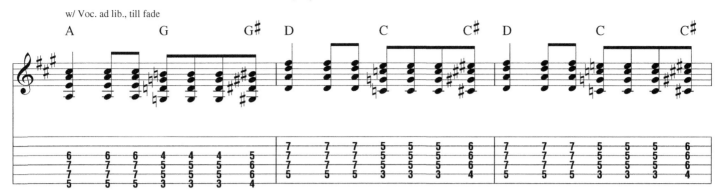

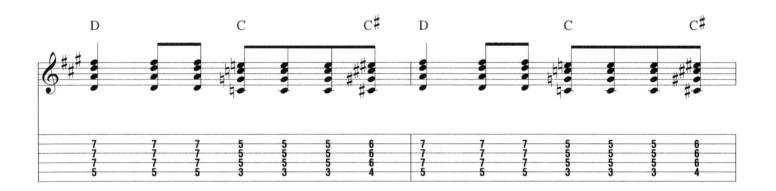

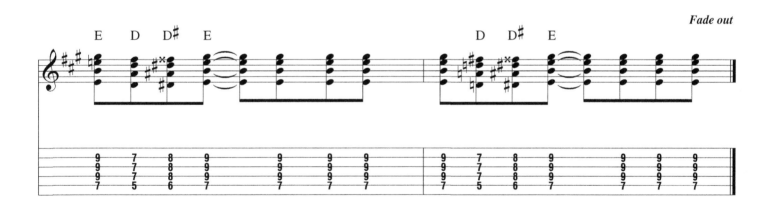

Additional Lyrics

2. Wake me, shake me, Mony, Mony.
   Shotgun, get it done. Come on, Mony.
   Don't 'cha stop cookin', it feels so good, yeah.
   Hey! Well, but don't stop now, hey,
   Come on, Mony. Well, come on, Mony.

Twist and Shout

Words and Music by Bert Russell and Phil Medley

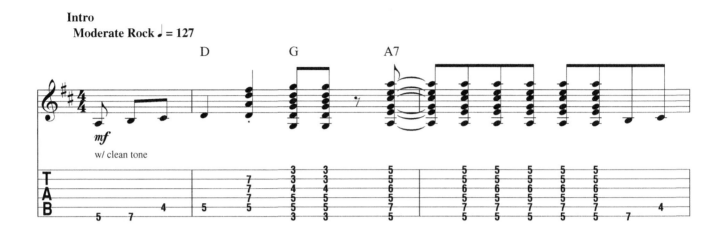

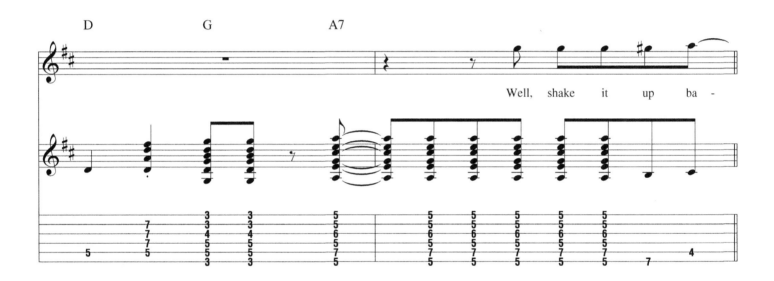

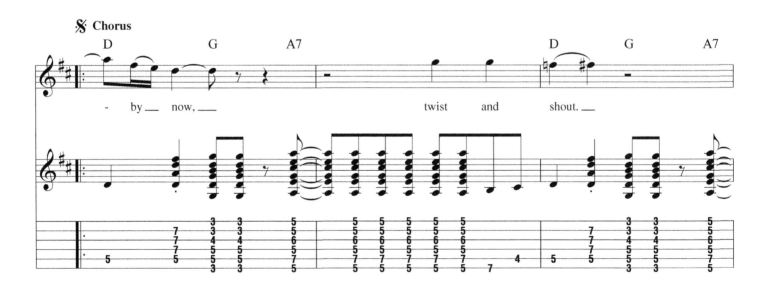

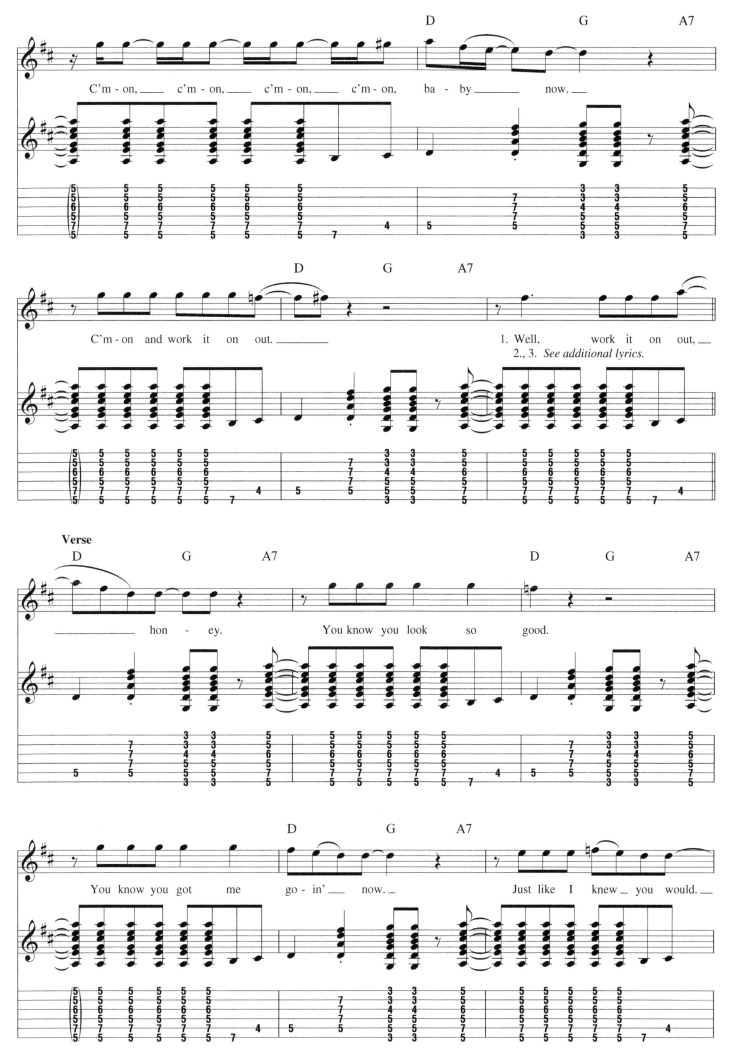

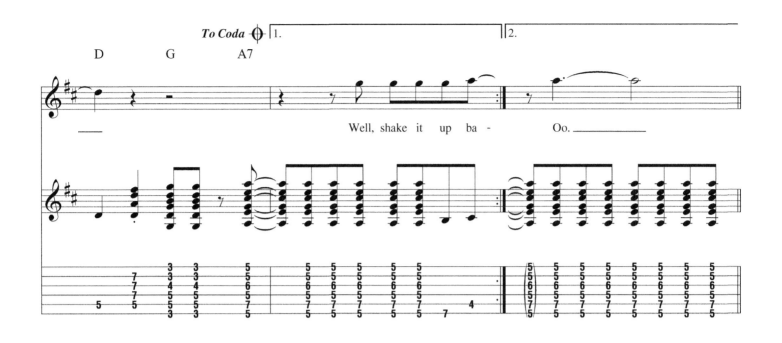

Well, shake it up ba - Oo. _____

Guitar Solo

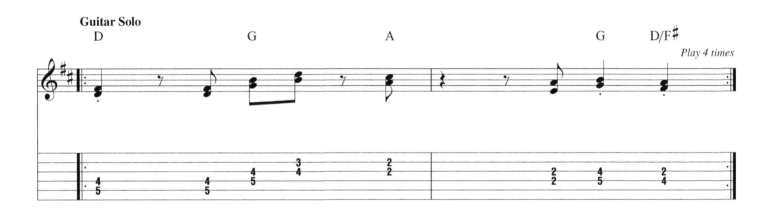

Bridge

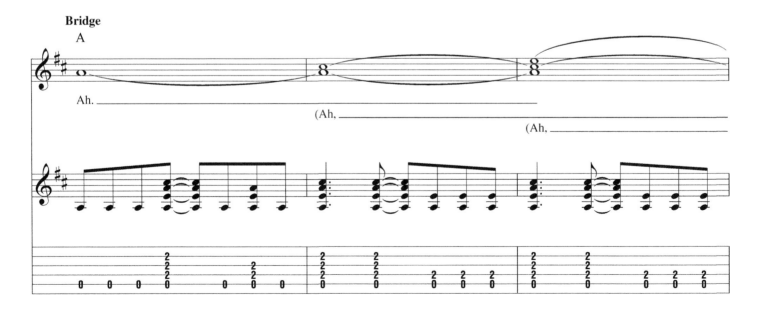

Ah. _____

(Ah, _____

(Ah, _____

Outro

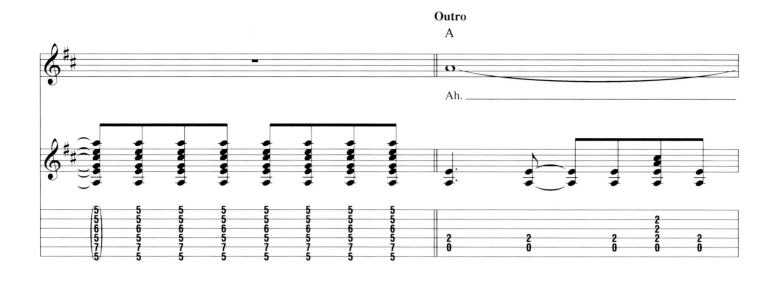

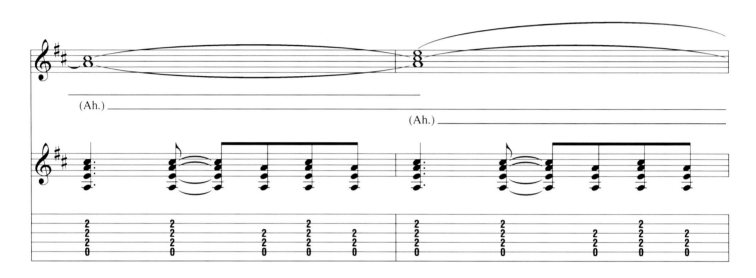

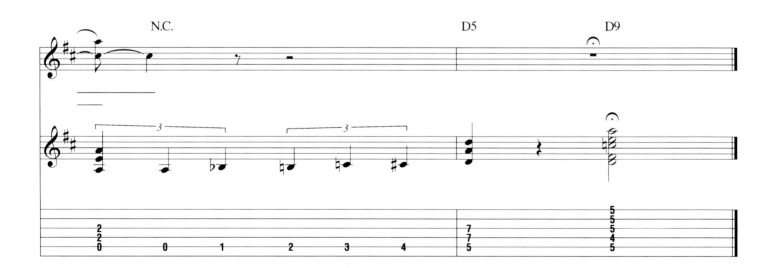

Additional Lyrics

2., 3. You know you're a twisty little girl.
You know you twist so fine.
C'mon and twist a little closer now.
And let me know that you're mine.
Oo.

Guitar Notation Legend

THE MUSICAL STAFF shows pitches and rhythms and is divided by bar lines into measures. Pitches are named after the first seven letters of the alphabet.

TABLATURE graphically represents the guitar fingerboard. Each horizontal line represents a string, and each number represents a fret.

4th string, 2nd fret   1st & 2nd strings open, played together   open D chord

HALF-STEP BEND: Strike the note and bend up 1/2 step.

WHOLE-STEP BEND: Strike the note and bend up one step.

GRACE NOTE BEND: Strike the note and bend up as indicated. The first note does not take up any time.

SLIGHT (MICROTONE) BEND: Strike the note and bend up 1/4 step.

BEND AND RELEASE: Strike the note and bend up as indicated, then release back to the original note. Only the first note is struck.

PRE-BEND: Bend the note as indicated, then strike it.

VIBRATO: The string is vibrated by rapidly bending and releasing the note with the fretting hand.

PALM MUTING: The note is partially muted by the pick hand lightly touching the string(s) just before the bridge.

HAMMER-ON: Strike the first (lower) note with one finger, then sound the higher note (on the same string) with another finger by fretting it without picking.

PULL-OFF: Place both fingers on the notes to be sounded. Strike the first note and without picking, pull the finger off to sound the second (lower) note.

LEGATO SLIDE: Strike the first note and then slide the same fret-hand finger up or down to the second note. The second note is not struck.

SHIFT SLIDE: Same as legato slide, except the second note is struck.

TRILL: Very rapidly alternate between the notes indicated by continuously hammering on and pulling off.

TAPPING: Hammer ("tap") the fret indicated with the pick-hand index or middle finger and pull off to the note fretted by the fret hand.

NATURAL HARMONIC: Strike the note while the fret-hand lightly touches the string directly over the fret indicated.

PINCH HARMONIC: The note is fretted normally and a harmonic is produced by adding the edge of the thumb or the tip of the index finger of the pick hand to the normal pick attack.

TREMOLO PICKING: The note is picked as rapidly and continuously as possible.

VIBRATO BAR DIVE AND RETURN: The pitch of the note or chord is dropped a specified number of steps (in rhythm) then returned to the original pitch.

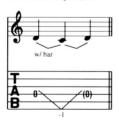

VIBRATO BAR SCOOP: Depress the bar just before striking the note, then quickly release the bar.

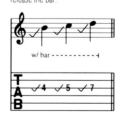

VIBRATO BAR DIP: Strike the note and then immediately drop a specified number of steps, then release back to the original pitch.

Additional Musical Definitions

 (accent)
- Accentuate note (play it louder)

 (staccato)
- Play the note short

D.S. al Coda
- Go back to the sign ($\%$), then play until the measure marked *"To Coda"*, then skip to the section labelled *"Coda."*

D.C. al Fine
- Go back to the beginning of the song and play until the measure marked *"Fine"* (end).

Fill
- Label used to identify a brief melodic figure which is to be inserted into the arrangement.

N.C.
- No Chord

- Repeat measures between signs.

 1.   2.
- When a repeated section has different endings, play the first ending only the first time and the second ending only the second time.

HAL•LEONARD GUITAR PLAY-ALONG

Complete song lists available online.

This series will help you play your favorite songs quickly and easily. Just follow the tab and listen to the audio to the hear how the guitar should sound, and then play along using the separate backing tracks. Audio files also include software to slow down the tempo without changing pitch. The melody and lyrics are included in the book so that you can sing or simply follow along.

INCLUDES TAB

Prices, contents, and availability subject to change without notice.

www.halleonard.com

0820
173